Little People, **BIG DREAMS**

MAYA ANGELOU

Little People, **BIG DREAMS**

MAYA ANGELOU

Written by
Lisbeth Kaiser

Illustrated by
Leire Salaberria

Frances Lincoln
Children's Books

Marguerite was born in the city of St. Louis. Her brother called her Maya. When Maya was four, she and her brother were sent to live with their grandmother in Stamps, Arkansas.

Growing up in the South, Maya was treated unfairly because of the color of her skin and because she was a girl. The world outside was very cruel.

Home was hard too. When Maya was eight, her mother's boyfriend attacked her. Maya was so upset, she stopped talking.

A friend of her grandmother's named Mrs. Flowers noticed that Maya was afraid to use her voice. Mrs. Flowers showed Maya all kinds of wonderful books, and how the words come alive when you read them out loud.

Maya found her voice again in the stories and poems of great writers. She loved words so much, she read every book in the library.

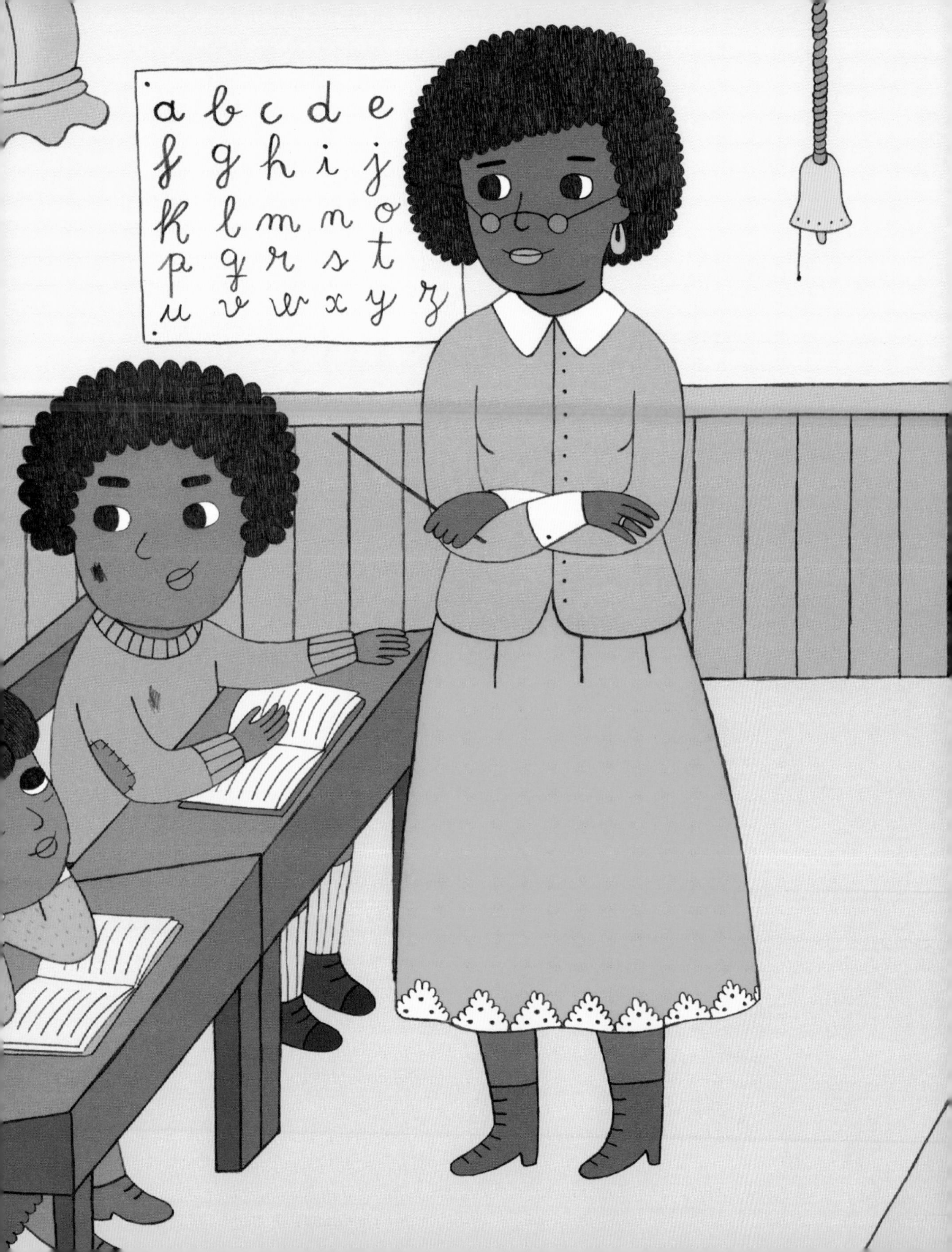
a b c d e
f g h i j
k l m n o
p q r s t
u v w x y z

Even though Maya was a great student, she was told that she couldn't get a good job because of the color of her skin.

"lift eve

But she had pride and hope. She thought,
"There's nothing I can't be."

voice "

And she was right.
She was a cook and a streetcar conductor.

She was a dancer, a singer, and an actress.

She traveled the world, and learned to speak a lot of languages.

At home in America, she worked to
help all people get treated equally.

It wasn't until Maya was all grown up that
she decided she wanted to be a writer.
So she began writing a book about her life.

She told the story of a little girl who struggled through hard times but didn't give up.

People all around the world were moved by her
powerful story and her beautiful words.

Maya became a famous writer, teacher, and speaker, inspiring everyone with her belief that you can be anything you want to be.

On the day Bill Clinton became president, Maya read a poem. She had once been a little girl who was afraid to use her voice. Now she was speaking to the entire country, about her favorite thing: hope.

MAYA ANGELOU

(Born 1928 • Died 2014)

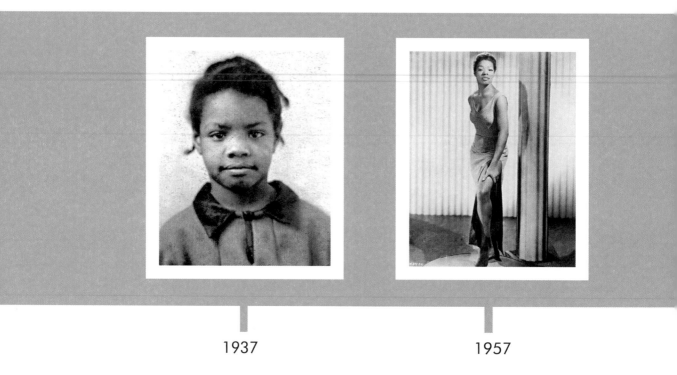

1937   1957

Maya Angelou is one of the most memorable voices in American
culture. Born Marguerite Annie Johnson in St. Louis, Missouri,
she spent much of her childhood in a small town in the South.
There, she faced a lot of unfairness because of her skin color.
When she was eight, she was attacked by her mother's boyfriend
and she stopped speaking for five years. In that time, she
grew to love books and found power and strength in words.
Maya overcame her childhood struggles and went on to lead
a marvelous life. She became a dancer, singer, actress, writer,
director, journalist, playwright, producer, teacher, and an activist

1971   1990

for civil rights. She performed in nightclubs, and began calling
herself Maya Angelou. She also became a mother and a
grandmother. In 1969, Maya turned the memories from her
childhood into a book called *I Know Why the Caged Bird Sings*.
The book became famous and sold millions of copies around
the world. Maya wrote many more books, won many awards,
and read her poems at the White House and the United Nations.
People everywhere continue to be inspired by her incredible life,
her beautiful words, and her powerful, hopeful voice.

Want to find out more about **Maya Angelou**?

She has written many great books herself, like:
Poetry for Young People: Maya Angelou edited by Dr. Edwin Graves Wilson
Ph.D, illustrated by Jerome Lagarrigue

You could also try these biographies:
Who Was Maya Angelou? by Ellen Labrecque, Dede Putra and Nancy Harrison
Maya Angelou: Journey of the Heart by Jayne Pettit

First published in the UK and the US in 2016 by Frances Lincoln Children's Books,
74–77 White Lion Street, London N1 9PF, UK
QuartoKnows.com
Visit our blogs at QuartoKnows.com

Commissioned as part of the Little People, Big Dreams series,
conceived by Mª Isabel Sánchez Vegara.
Originally published under the title Pequeña & Grande by Alba Editorial (www.albaeditorial.es)
Translation rights arranged by IMC Literary Agency

Maya Angelou™ is a trademark of Caged Bird Legacy, LLC. MayaAngelou.com
Text copyright © 2016 by Lisbeth Kaiser
Illustrations copyright © 2016 by Leire Salaberria

'Lift up your hearts' is a line taken from "On the Pulse of Morning" from ON THE PULSE OF MORNING by Maya
Angelou, copyright © 1993 by Maya Angelou. Used by permission of Random House, an imprint and division of
Penguin Random House LLC. All rights reserved.

A catalogue record for this book is available from the British Library.

ISBN 978-1-84780-889-9

Manufactured in Guangdong, China TT052018

11

MIX
Paper from
responsible sources
FSC® C016973

Photographic acknowledgements (pages 28-29, from left to right) 1. Photo and Maya Angelou™ is a trademark of Caged Bird Legacy, LLC.
MayaAngelou.com 2. Photo © Everett Collection Historical / Alamy Stock Photo 3. Photo © ASSOCIATED PRESS 4. Photo by: Universal History
Archive/UIG via Getty images

Also in the *Little People,* **BIG DREAMS** series:

FRIDA KAHLO

ISBN: 978-1-84780-783-0

Meet Frida Kahlo, one of the best artists of the twentieth century.

COCO CHANEL

ISBN: 978-1-84780-784-7

Discover the life of Coco Chanel, the famous fashion designer.

AMELIA EARHART

ISBN: 978-1-84780-888-2

Learn about Amelia Earhart—the first female to fly solo over the Atlantic.

AGATHA CHRISTIE

ISBN: 978-1-84780-960-5

Meet the queen of the imaginative mystery—Agatha Christie.

MARIE CURIE

ISBN: 978-1-84780-962-9

Be introduced to Marie Curie, the Nobel Prize-winning scientist.

ROSA PARKS

ISBN: 978-1-78603-018-4

Discover the life of Rosa Parks, the first lady of the civil rights movement.

EMMELINE PANKHURST

ISBN: 978-1-78603-020-7

Meet Emmeline Pankhurst, the suffragette who helped women get the vote.

AUDREY HEPBURN

ISBN: 978-1-78603-053-5

Learn about the iconic actress and humanitarian—Audrey Hepburn.

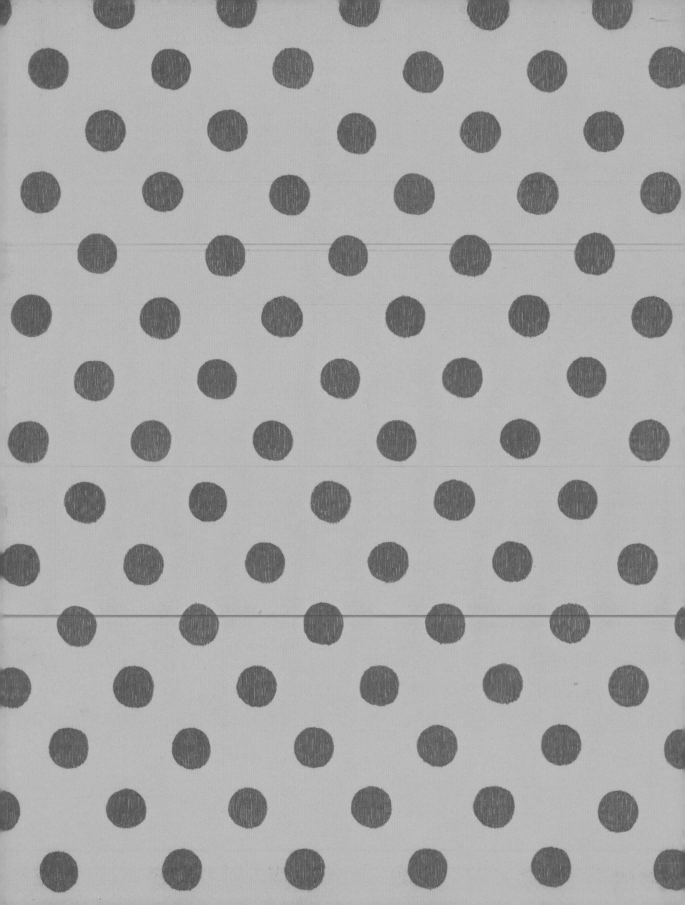